Rᴏɢᴇʀ MᴄGᴏᴜɢʜ was born in Liverpool, and received the Freedom of the City in 2001. President of the Poetry Society, he presents the popular Radio 4 programme *Poetry Please*, and has published many books for adults and children. In 2005 he received a CBE from the Queen for his services to literature.

www.rogermcgough.org.uk

Other books for children
by Roger McGough

ALL THE BEST
AN IMAGINARY MENAGERIE
ANOTHER CUSTARD PIE
BAD BAD CATS
CROCODILE TEARS
DOTTY INVENTIONS
EIGHTY POEMS
I NEVER LIKED WEDNESDAYS
IF ONLY WE HAD A HELICOPTER
LUCKY
MIND THE GAP
MONEY-GO-ROUND
MOONTHIEF
MY DAD'S A FIRE-EATER
NAILING THE SHADOW
NOAH'S ARK
PILLOW TALK
POETRY PIE
SKY IN THE PIE
SLAPSTICK
THE BEAST OF BABYLON
THE BEE'S KNEES
THE KITE AND CAITLIN
THE LIGHTHOUSE THAT RAN AWAY
THE MAGIC FOUNTAIN
THE STOWAWAYS
UNTIL I MET DUDLEY
YOU TELL ME (with Michael Rosen)

OVER to YOU!

ROGER McGOUGH

PUFFIN POETRY

PUFFIN BOOKS

UK | USA | Canada | Ireland | Australia
India | New Zealand | South Africa

Puffin Books is part of the Penguin Random House group of companies
whose addresses can be found at global.penguinrandomhouse.com.

www.penguin.co.uk
www.puffin.co.uk
www.ladybird.co.uk

First published 2022
001

Text copyright © Roger McGough, 2022
Illustrations © Jennifer Naalchigar, 2022
The moral right of the author and illustrator has been asserted

Set in 13/16pt Baskerville MT Std
Typeset by Jouve (UK), Milton Keynes
Text design by Arabella Jones
Printed and bound in Great Britain by Clays Ltd, Elcograf S.p.A.

The authorized representative in the EEA is Penguin Random House Ireland,
Morrison Chambers, 32 Nassau Street, Dublin D02 YH68

A CIP catalogue record for this book is available from the British Library

ISBN: 978-0-241-52760-3

All correspondence to:
Puffin Books
Penguin Random House Children's
One Embassy Gardens, 8 Viaduct Gardens
London SW11 7BW

Just take the words and run with them.
Young poet, it's over to you!

Contents

The Opening Poem   1

My First Poem . . .
Today I Am Writing My First Poem   5
Today I Am Writing My Second Poem   6
Today I Am Writing My Third Poem   7
This Poem is Punishment   8
A Poem to Help Make the World a Better Place   9
Today I Found a Simile on the Carpet   10
Schlimmbesserung   11
My First Haiku   12
My Second Haiku   13
Hooked on Haiku   14
Haiku Hygiene   15
A Word of Warning about Words   16
No Going Back   17
Today I Am Writing a New Poem   18
Today I Will Finish the Poem I Started Yesterday   19
This Was Meant to Be My Final Poem   20

. . . Over to You!
The Rhinoceros Dreams of Becoming an Airline Pilot 25
The Cat Dreams of Becoming a Racing Driver   26
The Rabbit Dreams of the Open Seas   28
The Badger Dreams of That Final Bout   30
The Wasp Speaks Out in Defence   32

Once Upon a Bicycle   34
Who Was the Girl?   36
Mischief and Beans   38
Starfish *Enterprise*   39
Vlad the Impala   40
Skip Skip Hooray!   41
The Battle of Trafalgar Square   42
The Good Ship *Attenborough*   44
Alphabet Soup   46
More Alphabet Soup, Anyone?   49
An Angel in the Library   50
Well-mannered Poetry   52
Wild Stallions   54
At Home on the Range   56
Performance Poet   57
Out There   58
Well After Dark   60
Not So Well After Dark   61
A Cautionary Tale   62
Anybody There?   63
DIY Valentine Card   64
The Perfect Day   65
Everyday Birthday Day   66
Feeble Excuses   68
The Puzzle Tree   70
A Few Questions About Eternity   72
Without Eternity Where Are We?   74
Beating the Bugs   75
Nonner   76

I Am Done with Shade   77
Drums on Legs   78
I'm Nicer Than I Look   80
I'm Not as Nice as I Look   81
Six Impossible Things to Do Before Breakfast   82
Silly Old Cat   84
The Golden Retriever   85
Midnight in the Ice Rink   86
Three Cheers for the Cheerleaders   88
The Poetry Olympics   90
Tobogganing in Tobago   91
Granma's Gooseberry Jam   92
Rich   94
Money-go-round   96
Now You Are Grown-up   97
When You Grow Up   98
Let Us Know   100
The Last Christmas Tree   102
The Veggie Table   104
The Runaway Sprout   106
The Christmas Sound Collector   108

The Closing Poem   113

Acknowledgements   115
Author Acknowledgements   117
Index of Poems   119
Index of First Lines   123

The Opening Poem

This is the opening poem,
The one that sets the tone,
That lights up the sky like a rocket
(Or in this case, sinks like a   )
                              stone

This is the opening poem
And it's going badly wrong.
It's not clever or funny, but luckily
It's only three verses long

That was the opening poem,
The one that says 'hello'.
Sorry to waste your time.
Now over the page you go.

My FIRST POEM...

Today I Am Writing My First Poem

Today I am writing my first poem
and I am very excited.

I don't know what it is about yet
because I haven't got to the end.

Teacher says just keep going
until the poem tells you otherwise.

I can hear its voice now: far off,
coming closer. '*Enough!*' it cries. '*Stop! Stop!*'

Today I Am Writing
My Second Poem

I am writing my second poem
Even though my first one
Made me promise I wouldn't.

Teacher says keep on writing.
It is the journey that is exciting
Not the destination.

I'm not so sure.
When the journey is over
I'm going back to PlayStation.

Today I Am Writing
My Third Poem

I am writing my third poem
Because I can't get my big sister
And her silly friends off the PlayStation.

Did you notice in my second poem
That I rhymed 'writing' with 'exciting',
And 'destination' with 'PlayStation'?
I didn't mean to – it just happened.

Teacher says that poems don't have to rhyme
But when they do the repetition of the same sound
Can be pleasing to the ear. Who cares?

Oh, good. I can hear my silly sister
And her big friends going upstairs.

This Poem is Punishment

I am writing this poem
Because Teacher said I had to.
It was either that or detention.

For what? Gazing out of the window
When I should have been paying attention?
To what? Sums that don't add up?

I wouldn't mind, but I wasn't gazing
Out of the window but into my head
Where the good stuff happens.

Teacher said that imagination
was like thinking outside of the box.
Isn't the classroom a box?

Isn't gazing out of the window
Like thinking outside of the box?
Next time, I'll take detention.

A Poem to Help Make the World a Better Place

I wanted to write a poem
And I knew what I wanted to say.

It would help bring people together
And I worked on it night and day.

My heart was in the right place,
But the words, they got in the way.

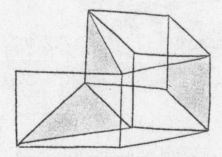

Today I Found a Simile on the Carpet

For homework I have to write a poem.
Therefore I am at home writing a poem.

Teacher says it must contain a simile.
I am confused. What is a simile?*

As I write this, Coco the cat
is lying on the carpet purring,

like a poem waiting to be stroked.

When you say a thing is like another thing, that is a simile.

Schlimmbesserung

Yesterday Teacher made the class
write that down. It took ages.

It means fiddling with something
in the hope of making it better

only to end up by making it worse.
(Just one word for all that!)

It is a German word, which is good
because now I can speak German.

Teacher said that when we do a painting
or write a poem we should know when to stop.

Like now.

My First Haiku

This is the first time
I have written a haiku*.
(Which proves I can count.)

* *Japanese haiku contain seventeen syllables spread across three lines: 5/7/5.*

My Second Haiku

This haiku was closed
until you, the reader, came
and opened it. Ta.

Hooked on Haiku

A word of warning:
Haiku can be addictive.
You write one and then

on ly se ven teen
syll a bles la ter you want
to write an o ther.

Haiku Hygiene

After reading this
remember to wash your hands.
Coronavirus.

A Word of Warning about Words

Give a word an inch and it will take a mile.
What starts off as a harmless little haiku
ends up as a difficult sonnet* or, worse still,
one of those poems that goes on and on and on and on.

Having been invited to a party
words want to enjoy themselves
and will outstay their welcome
until you step in and put your foot down.

Uninvited words, gatecrashers
and hangers-on can ruin everything.
Throw them out before it gets out of hand.
It's your poem, remember – not theirs.

* *A sonnet has fourteen lines and so many rules that Teacher says you need a poetic licence to be able to write one.*

No Going Back

Once you start writing poems
there is no going back.

They chase after you.
You write one, leave it there,

and weeks later it will slide up
demanding attention.

Like a needy cat?
No, been there. Done that.

Like a phone that needs charging?
Table that needs clearing?

Homework that needs finishing?
Big sister that needs PlayStation?

OK, we get the idea – now give it a rest.

Today I Am Writing a New Poem

So far, so good

Today I Will Finish the Poem
I Started Yesterday

So far, so good, as far as I can tell.
No idea where it's going, but it's going quite well.
It's about a girl called Akira and I hardly know her
So it's sworn to secrecy and I'll never show her.

She is very laid-back, softly spoken and shy
(Which poems can be too), and that is why
When the bell goes in a minute and lessons begin,
This one is going straight into the bin.

This Was Meant to Be My Final Poem

This was meant to be my final poem,
A letter of goodbye, short, sharp
And funny, which began '*Dear Poetry,*

Please don't be offended.
But what's the point? You're boring.
We're finished. It's ended.'

And then a strange thing happened.
Out of nowhere (well, Syria actually)
A new girl joined the class.

English is her second language.
Softly spoken and very shy,
But the poems she writes!

Like watching the news on TV,
Bombs and guns, smoke and tears,
And Akira in the middle of it all.

And that's why this isn't my final poem.
Her words, simple and full of pain,
Make you want to change the world.

So maybe I can write poems
Not as good as hers, but ones that
Put their shoulders to the wheel.

Big ask. I have no idea how to do it.
But I'll find a way. And I won't tell Teacher.
It'll be my little secret (and Akira's). OK?

...OVER to YOU!

The Rhinoceros Dreams of Becoming an Airline Pilot

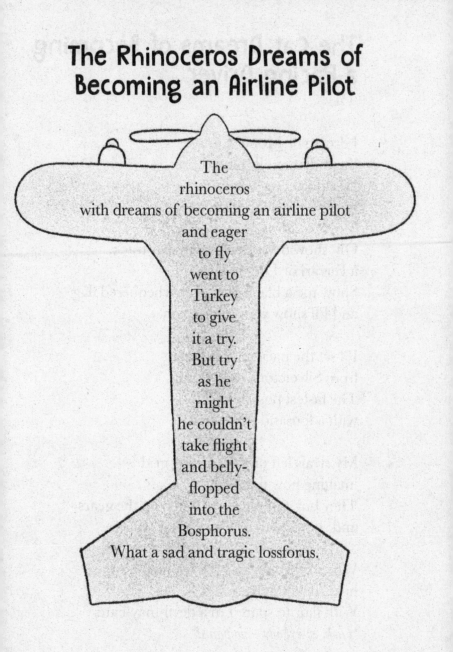

The
rhinoceros
with dreams of becoming an airline pilot
and eager
to fly
went to
Turkey
to give
it a try.
But try
as he
might
he couldn't
take flight
and belly-
flopped
into the
Bosphorus.
What a sad and tragic lossforus.

The Cat Dreams of Becoming a Racing Driver

I dream of Monte Carlo,
the Indianapolis Grand Prix,
Winning every trophy,
my mean machine and me.

Oh, show me a track, a circular track,
a Ferrari or Lotus Elan.
Show me a black-and-white chequered flag
and I'll show you a champion.

I'll set the pace in every race,
from Silverstone to Le Mans.
The fastest puss in history
with a fousand feline fans.

My rivals left on the starting grid
imagine how that feels.
They burst into tears as I step up the gears,
and show them a clean pair of wheels.

When I throttle past the winning post,
hear the almighty roars,
With flair to spare I'm a devil-may-care.
'Look, everybody – no paws!'

Oh, give me a car, a racing car, a Maserati or Lotus Elan
Show me a 10,000cc engine with back-thrust overdrive,
super-charged megathingies, ultra-gear suspension divits,
And I'll show you a happy . . . CRASH . . . *Meeeeooooow!*

The Rabbit Dreams of the Open Seas

Sailing, they say, is a wonderful life:
To hop aboard and sail whenever you can,
Take each day and never stop to plan
As the prow cuts through the water like a knife.

All my worries left behind upon the shore.
Casting off, and suddenly I'm free.
Just the sky, a gentle breeze and the sea.
Could a bunny ask for anything more?

Don't get me wrong, I know where I belong:
In a field with other rabbits by the score.
But a busy bunny's life can be a chore,
So I dream of boats and sing a boating song.

Sailing daily if I could, in a dinghy made of wood,
a canoe, skiff or coracle, a kayak, or, if not,
a pedalo, gondola, schooner or a yacht
(Even a raft made by otters would be good).

Life in a warren can feel quite foreign
To a gentle soul who dreams of open seas.
To escape life's busy burrow I would run away tomurrow
For the freedom to do just as I please.

As the prow cuts through the water like a knife.
As the prow cuts through the water like a knife.

The Badger Dreams of That Final Bout

Now you wouldn't think to look at me
All grizzled, fat and slow,
That I used to be a boxing champ
Many, many years ago.

I was a world-class middleweight
When my fur had a youthful gloss.
In this neck of the neighbourhood
'Bulldog' Badger was the boss.

I had such a reputation.
Seems like only yesterday
That folk would come from miles and miles
Just to keep out of my way.

There's good badgers and bad badgers.
I was somewhere in between.
At home in the sett, a loving dad.
In the ring? Boy, was I mean!

Of course I've been beaten
Lots of times and ended up on the floor,
But I learned the lesson Granpa taught
And always came back for more.

But now I'm old, and my eyes are dim.
I'm still in training for that final bout
When I'll dream of all the good times
As I'm slowly counted out.

The Wasp Speaks Out in Defence

Z-Z-Z-sorry I stung you, I don't know what it is.
My hearts starts a-pumpin', and my head gets in a tizzZZ.
My wings start a-knockin', and my eyes start to glaze.
Z-Z-Z-suddenly it's one of those days.

Z-Z-Z-something comes over me, I fall into a trance
As if a wicked fairy leads me into the dance.
The music takes me over; it drives me insane.
Z-Z-Z-suddenly here it comes again.

Z-Z-Z-something comes over me as if from outer space
When I least expect it like a pie in the face.
Don't take it personally. I didn't pick on you.
Z-Z-Z-stinging is what yellow jackets* do.

Z-Z-Z-something comes over me and lands me in a mess.
Though I'm a precious species, a fact I'd like to stress,
Mums don't sting for fun – we're protecting our young.
Z-Z-Z-so bear that in mind the next time you're stung.

ZZZZZZZzz

* The yellow jacket (or Vespula as they are known in posh circles) is the most common species of wasp to be found in Europe. Only the females sting and then only in defence of their young. Wasps are busy predators of pest insects and therefore important for the environment.

Once Upon a Bicycle

Once upon a bicycle
We set off for the beach.
Only seven miles away
So well within our reach

(Or so we thought).

Reckoned on a couple of hours,
It took all day.
Two punctures, one collision
Before we lost our way.

A chain came off, the sun beat down,
Flora got stung by a bee,
Harry swerved to avoid a cat
And head-longed into a tree.

Deserted beach, distant thunder.
Not exactly what we'd planned,
As dehydrated and exhausted
We collapsed upon the sand.

The ride back was even worse.
You'd laugh if you'd have seen us.
The rain came down, the night grew dark
And not a light between us.

No mobile phones in those days.
Prayer was all we had.
The police were sympathetic
But Mum and Dad went mad.

Sunburnt and saddle-sore
Next day did I feel rough.
Once upon a bicycle
was more than enough.

Who Was the Girl?

Who was the naughty girl I saw
combing her hair with a bluebell?
Paying her fare with a seashell?
Sawing the see-saw in two?

Who was the cheeky girl I saw
spreading butter on a yoga mat?
Hiding the pizza in Granma's hat?
Picking the pocket of a kangaroo?

Who was the silly girl I saw
asking an octopus to dance?
Filling her brother's pants with ants?
No word of a lie, this is true.

Who was the giddy girl I saw
putting the cart before the horse?
Painting her nails with tomato sauce?
High-fiving a lion at the zoo?

Who was the crazy girl I saw
surfing on a tea tray?
Dancing with a duvet?
Flushing my poems down the loo?

Who was the naughty girl I saw
doing all these crazy things and more?
The joker we love and can't ignore
The girl we despair of but always adore
That girl, of course, was YOU!

Mischief and Beans

Be warned: today I feel strong and agile.
If there's a gong or a badge, I'll
win it. Run half a mile in a minute.
Show me a mountain, for example,
and while others scramble, slip and flop,
watch me whoosh straight to the top.

I have so much energy I could burst.
There isn't a race where I couldn't come first.
Challenge me to a fight, you'll regret it.
If a lion attacked, I would pet it.
Show me a fence and I'll clear it
as the sun cheers me on. Can you hear it?

Today I have so much pep and vim
I could tear a triceratops limb from limb,
deflect a tsunami, defeat a huge army.
That ugly block at the end of our street?
I'd flatten it using my hands and bare feet.

Don't laugh. You may be bigger than me,
but as the sun is my witness I'm fit as a flea.
The naughtiest in class, full of mischief and beans,
(imagine this girl when she reaches her teens!)

Starfish *Enterprise*

A starfish stranded upon the shore
Looked up at the night sky and liked what she saw:

A million starfish gazing down
Each one wearing a glittering crown.

She sighed. 'How I'd like to be
spread-eagled beside that milky blue sea

In silver dress with friends galore,
Not stretched out alone on a cold, cold shore.'

* * *

This starfish, though, was enterprising.
One mighty wish and she was rising,

Crashing through the sound barrier
As far into space as a wish could carry her.

Now twinkling nightly on display
In a starfish colony in the Milky Way.

Vlad the Impala*

I'm Vlad the Impala
Leader of the herd.
Despite what you hear
No need to be scared.

I'm not a tyrant
Bloodthirsty and mad.
I'm an antelope
And my name is Vlad.

---

* *Not to be confused with Vlad the Impaler, a cruel monarch born in Transylvania in 1431.*

Skip Skip Hooray!

Give an antelope a skipping rope
And it will skip all day.

Then slope into the bush and mope
When you take the rope away.

The Battle of
Trafalgar Square

There is something strange about Trafalgar Square.
Someone is missing who should be there.

Who is that sailor, stern and solemn?
'Tis Lord Nelson down from his column.

What nightmare vision brought him down?
The sight of rubbish all over town.

One eye, one arm, one aim in mind:
To leave a cleaner world behind.

All over the country at his request
Litter pickers do their best.

Unlocked at last, and free to roam,
Intent on cleaning up our home.

On mountain paths and motorways,
On coastal walks they spend the days

Cleaning up. Good citizens prepared to fight
A war with *Victory* not yet in sight.

And so for the admiral and his volunteers
Let's all give three hearty cheers.

* * *

Now you've read this poem, I would implore,
Don't crumple it up and chuck on the floor!

The Good Ship Attenborough

There's excitement in Antarctica:
a saviour is on the way,
Half man, half ship, in coat of red,
who vows to save the day.

A man of steel, with heart of gold
and brain the size of Hyde Park,
Rides the flood like Noah
on a recommissioned ark.

With damage to the environment
and global warming on his mind
The mission, not yet impossible,
to save the planet and mankind.

Not for money, power or glory,
plain truth the only prize,
There's expectation in the deep
and excitement in the skies.

Beneath the melting ice,
dolphins, seals and whales
Swim round and round in circles,
clapping fins and wagging tails.

Penguins prance and pirouette
and all the birds of the air
Keep their feathers crossed
as they offer up a prayer

For the good ship *Attenborough**
and the scientists on board
Who will bring to light the evidence
that cannot be ignored.

Only then can we leave the Earth
a healthier, safer place
For the sake of those who depend on us
and the future of our race.

The sea is rising, the message is clear.
Have we time to rewind the clock?
Shhh . . . listen. What do we hear?
Antarc tic . . . toc . . . *tic . . . toc . . . tic . . .*
     tock . . . tick . . . tock . . . tick . . .

* *The polar research vessel was launched by Sir David Attenborough in Birkenhead on Merseyside, July 2018.*

Alphabet Soup

Answers are Questions' best friends (until they get one wrong)

Bathroom scales dread the *thump-thump* of smelly feet along the landing

Crumbs are cake's cast-offs

Dolls in doll's houses dream of selling up and hitting the road

Empty buckets in the desert are soon filled with hot air

Few fortune tellers are fortunate enough to make fortunes

Garlic-scented perfume at only £5 a bottle. Not to be sniffed at

Helen of Troy dressed like a boy, just to annoy

Italics, so lazy they can't be bothered to stand up straight

Jumping for joy always ends up on the floor

Kettles boil only when the bubbles tell it to

Lips that love to smile live longest

Mirrors are good at faces but terrible at names

Next-door neighbours? That's us: next-door neighbours'
next-door neighbours

Odd numbers spend half their lives trying to get even

Paint goes shy when people pause to watch it dry

Quicksand is ideal if you need to build a castle in a hurry

Round the rugged rocks the ragged rascals dropped litter

Suitcases become heavy only when lifted

Tin soldiers are no match for enemy magnets

Undercover agents are hopeless at getting out of bed in
the morning

Volume is happiest when heard and not seen

Waves still splashing about on the beach well past midnight

Xmas stockings look forward to putting their feet up on
  Boxing Day

Yo-yos in dusty cupboards discuss life's ups and downs

Zero? Nothing much going for it really. Zilch.

More Alphabet Soup, Anyone?

I had alphabet soup for lunch

and found W o r m s in it.

I also found beans, carrots,

an eyeball, socks and onions.

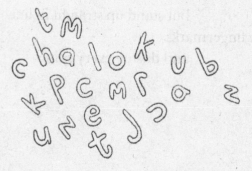

An Angel in the Library

The books in the library
                    shuffle on the shelves
The pages all aflutter
                    talk among themselves
The colours on the covers
                    slowly fade to grey
On hearing that someone
                    is leaving them today

That *someone* must be special
                    to explain all the tears
Someone who cared for
                    and loved them down the years
Who taught them not to slouch
                    but stand up straight in line
Removed dirty fingermarks
                    and dusted every spine

Who rearranged the authors' names
                    to read from A to Z
And sang a gentle lullaby
                    when it was time for bed
Who made a fuss of visitors
                    every little girl or boy
And chose the perfect book
                    each reader might enjoy

Well-known illustrators
                    would often come to call
And couldn't leave until they'd left
                    a drawing on the wall
Who is the special someone
                    that all the books admire?
The guardian angel of the library
                    has chosen to retire.

(And how does an ex-librarian fill the empty days?
By writing books about how books continue to amaze.)

Well-mannered Poetry

Poetry should have good manners
Aiming to pacify and to please
Regardless of race or gender
Putting readers at their ease.

I want mine to lead by example
At a thoughtful and gentle pace
The syllables carefully counted
Each word knowing its place.

I want to bring my poems up properly
To be decent, modest and kind
Helping those who find it a struggle
To explore the landscape of the mind.

Poetry should be seen and not heard
Soul music for the inner ear
Its voice never harsh or strident
But bell-like, soothing and clear.

Poems should avoid the limelight.
Delicate, they are things of rare beauty
Not to be flaunted or streamed online.
To protect them is our duty.

I hope this advice comes in useful
(*Though most of it's not really true*).
Just take the words and run with them.
Young poet, it's over to you.

Wild Stallions

I wish my poems used bad language
Not afraid to get up and fight

Instead of mumbling in the darkness
Jump on stage, grab the mic and recite

I wish my poems would point fingers
Exposing the liars and fools

I wish they would run free like wild stallions
Instead of being tethered like mules.

I wish my poems would go crazy
Hold parties for kids in the street

Instead of serenading the moon
Go dancing on Mars in bare feet

I wish my poems would play dirty
Speak out and break all the rules

I wish they would run free like wild stallions
Instead of being tethered like mules.

I wish my poems had loud voices
Not be afraid to raise them and shout

Bring shame on the trolls and the bullies
Name them and drive them all out

I wish my poems would get angry
Go on strike and lay down their tools

I wish they would run free like wild stallions
Instead of being tethered like mules.

I wish my poems would stay youthful
Not grow older and wiser with age

Seek adventure out in the real world
Not confined to the comfort of the page

I wish my poems were too dangerous
To be published or recited in schools

I wish they'd run free like wild stallions
Instead of being tethered like mules.

At Home on the Range

Words running wild don't make sense
A poet rounds them up, builds a fence
Takes the sounds and puts them through their paces
Some are sad and some wear smiley faces

Some are short but pack a punch
and some are quiet and shy
Some always give a hundred per cent
while others just don't try

Some are fit and push themselves
while others are simply lazy
Some can't help but tell the truth
while others are shiftless and hazy

The poet is a cowboy
Out on the range with the herds
Rounding them up at the close of day
And the horses, of course, are words.

Performance Poet

Not an astronaut or a scientist,
Not a chef or a vet, and certainly
NOT a teacher. When I grow up
I want to be a performance poet.

I've seen them on YouTube and stuff.
The way they move about
As the words come soaring out,
So cool, confident and athletic.

Trouble is, I'm not cool, and as for
Moving about, Wayne and my sister giggle
As the words come pouring out.
'Stop!' they yell. 'You're pathetic!'

But I have a plan. It will be the poetry
that performs, not me. I will just stand
on stage, close my eyes and set
the language loose on the crowd.

If it doesn't work, it won't be my fault.
I can blame the poems. I can't wait.
All I need now is a catchy stage name
(and another two hundred poems).

Out There

What is it like out there?
Is it raining cats and dogs?

No, only pups and kittens
And tiny ones at that

Then you don't need gloves or mittens
But you'd better take a hat.

* * *

What is it like out there?
Is the mist lingering still?

It's now a blanket of fog
And dirty, why do you ask?

Because if you go for a jog
You had better wear a mask.

* * *

What is it like out there?
Is the sun cracking the flags?

Yes, lolling all over the place
As if it could do no wrong

Then put lots of cream on your face.
And don't lie out too long.

* * *

What is it like out there?
Why is the wind going *shhh*?

Because the snow is falling
And no one is about

Out There, I hear it calling
Grab your coat and let's go out.

Well After Dark

Wednesday evening, well after dark,
In need of fresh air I went to the park.

The moon winked warmly as if to say
Glad you came, what game shall we play?

We passed the parcel with the stars
(The prize for the winner, a trip to Mars!).

We played Simon Says, Hide-and-Seek.
Can't wait to go again next week.

I've never had so much fun in the park.
Take my advice: go out after dark.

Not So Well After Dark

Thursday evening, well after dark,
In need of fresh air I went to the park.

Spat at by a goblin, stung by a snake,
Chased by a ghost risen up from the lake.

Pausing for breath, I stopped by the wood.
A vampire unfolded and sucked my blood.

Trees shook their fists, cursed and hissed.
A cloud threw a rock that narrowly missed.

Attacked by an alligator, bitten by a shark.
Take my advice: don't go out after dark.

A Cautionary Tale

This morning I threw caution to the wind.

Unfortunately the wind dropped suddenly
And caution crashed to the ground.

I tried to put it together again
But, like Humpty, it couldn't be put.
So I threw the pieces into Grandad's shed,
Making sure the door was shut.

Now I'm off in search of adventure,
Headstrong and devil-may-care,
Impetuous and reckless.
Come and join me if you dare!

Anybody There?

There are times when I feel I'm not real
Not made out of flesh, but thin air
Surrounded by friends who don't notice
Listen or let alone care.

When I told my teacher this morning
She turned and said, 'Anybody there?'

DIY Valentine Card

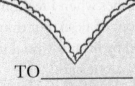

TO_____

Here's a card from your greatest admirer
With a love that is constant and true
A reminder that somewhere nearby
There's someone special for you

Someone who will do your bidding
And agree with all you say
Who was there at the very beginning
And who will never walk away.

From me to you, or you to me,
Either way it's the same.
A card from your greatest admirer,
Simply sign it with your name.

FROM_____

The Perfect Day

It was a disappointing day all round.
Friends hadn't learned the script,
The weather couldn't be bothered,
Even your body seemed disinterested.

And you were so looking forward to it.
Days, we demand too much of them,
But don't worry – a special one
will turn up when least expected.

Not a birthday, not the day out,
not the one you've been planning
and looking forward to for ages,
but one that begins like any other.

No ice cream involved or funfair rides,
Nothing to unwrap. No monsters slain
or battles won. Apart from making
someone smile, almost nothing happens.

And at the end of it,
as your smile sinks into the pillow,
and the inklings of a good dream take shape,
you hear it whisper, 'I have been the perfect day.'

Everyday Birthday Day

It was my birthday yesterday.
I had a party. It was great.
Lots of prezzies, loads to eat,
And it went on really late.

The only thing that spoiled it
(Apart from a punch-up with Wayne)
Was having to wait another year
Before I could do it again.

If I could make a wish come true
How about this for an idea?
To celebrate it every day
Instead of once a year?

Party games and singalongs,
More food than we can eat,
(Wayne saying sorry)
And Mum run off her feet.

If it was my birthday every day,
Tomorrow I'd be *two thousand
nine hundred and twenty-one*.
(Wow. All those candles!)

Feeble Excuses

I'm sorry this card arrived so late . . .

But on my way to the postbox
I was attacked by an angry mail-eating fox

As I fought it off and ran down the street
a python wrapped itself round my feet

I dragged myself clear, then what should appear
but a grizzly bear with a burning spear

Would nobody get me out of this mess?
I screamed for help, and then . . . success!

An old lady who happened to be driving past
stopped her car, so I hopped in fast

But soon I was in for a nasty surprise
when the lady turned out to be a wolf in disguise

Too late I realized as we drove into the wood
I should never have worn that red riding hood

Then, would you believe, my trousers caught fire!
The wolf pushed me out as the flames grew higher

A fire engine arrived, followed no less
by an armed police squad and the SAS,
Florence Nightingale, Cinderella, Goldilocks,
two brass bands and a film crew.

But enough of me and my feeble excuses.
Happy Birthday!

The Puzzle Tree

If I could choose, what tree would I be?
Not sturdy Oak or lofty Pine
Too gentrified for me

They seem to own the land
On which they stand. (Stood
In their shadow I think you'd agree)

Poplars are popular, and Firs first class
Ash cut a dash, and a Silver Birch
Is worth the search any day

A Willow, its branches sweeping low
Like a ballerina taking a bow
Can take the breath away

Conference, Bramley, Granny Smith
Apple and Pear trees take some beating
Each fall, their gifts, ours for the eating

Horse Chestnuts have the best nuts
(Although not to be eaten)
Playing conkers at school I couldn't be beaten

While the Holly has more thorns
Hawthorns have much to be admired
And I'm fired at the sight of a flowering Cherry

Towering Christmas trees make me merry
While Hornbeams by babbling streams
Provide the backdrop to restful dreams

So Hazel, Lime, Linden, Yew,
Beech, Elm? What tree would I be?
I'll give you a clue . . .

Next year I'll be one hundred and two!

Answer _ _ _ _ _

Answer: elder.

A Few Questions About Eternity

(i)

How quiet was it before the Big Bang?
Did it come as a surprise
or had there been rumblings?

(ii)

Was the beginning always there
or did it start when the banging
had stopped?

(iii)

Were humans around to notice
or did they come later?
Did they know it was later?

(iv)

When later became the present
how long before they noticed?
How soon did it become the past?

(v)

Will all things come to an end
with another Big Bang?
Or will that be just another beginning?

(vi)

Ask yourself, would you want to live forever?
Me? No, I haven't got the time.

Without Eternity Where Are We?

If *Eternity*
has no beginning and no end,
shouldn't it be *ternit*?

But if *ternit*
has no beginning and no end,
shouldn't it be *erni*?

And if *erni*
has no beginning and no end,
shouldn't it be *rn*?

And if *rn*
has no beginning and no end,
where are we?

Beating the Bugs

   (i)   Cover your mouth when you cough

   (ii)   Cover your nose when you sneeze

  (iii)   Cover your knees in custard

  (iv)   Cover your head when you freeze

   (v)   Wash your hands when you've been to the loo

  (vi)   Wash them before every mealtime too

 (vii)   If you must shout, shout quietly

(viii)   Avoid stuffy overcrowded places

  (ix)   And remember: bugs hate smiling faces

   (x)   xxxxxxxxxxxxxxxxxxxxxxxxxxxxxxxxxxxxx

Nonner

A nonner, what a nonner
I've been given by the Queen.
I wear the biggest medal
The world has ever seen.

It's made of solid silver
The size of a baby's head
Instead of my old teddy bear
It goes with me to bed.

Said Her Majesty:
'You may keep it *in perpetua.*'
(Which means it's mine forever.)
Are you jealous? I bet you are.

I Am Done with Shade

I am done with shade
Now I walk in the light
Smiling and unafraid

I have put paid
To thoughts that go bump in the night
I am done with shade

I will lead the parade
On a horse dazzling white
I am done with shade

Upon those who wish to be obeyed
I will wee from a great height
Smiling and unafraid

Up for the fight
Smiling and unafraid
I am done with shade.

Drums on Legs

When I'm dancing
I forget everything.
The beat takes me over

I sing
I'm the singer
I strum the air
I'm the lead guitar
Ba-bum-bum-bum
I'm the bass
But most of all
I'm the drummer

I'm the drums
Drums on legs
The drums
Drums on legs
The drums
Drums on legs
The drums
Drums on legs
The drums
Drums on legs
The drums
Drums on legs.

When the music stops
It's so quiet
I can hear myself
Sweating.

I'm Nicer Than I Look

I may be hairy and smelly
And covered in all kinds of muck
But underneath I'm nicer
Much nicer than I look

I could be mistaken for a robber
Or a low-life two-timing crook
But you can trust me with your money
I'm much nicer than I look

I may seem fierce and angry
Come at you like a runaway truck
But deep down I'm much nicer
Much nicer than I look

Some say I'm the horriblest
Most monstrous thing in the book
But, honest, I'm much nicer
Much nicer than I look.

I'm Not as Nice as I Look

I may look nice on the cover
But once you open the book
You may be surprised to discover
I'm not as nice as I look

You could mistake me for a princess
With my flowing golden tresses
Eyes that shine like sapphires
And expensive handmade dresses

I may look sweet and friendly
Full of charm and calm as can be
But inside I'm a raging inferno
A dark and stormy sea

My followers are my subjects
My kingdom is Instagram
A whirlwind of contradictions
A werewolf dressed as lamb

The one with my face on the cover
Please may I borrow that book?
But don't expect me to return it
I'm not as nice as I look.

Six Impossible Things to Do Before Breakfast

Make fresh orange juice using only lemons and Jaffa Cakes

Lightly poach Humpty Dumpty without breaking his shell

Pick mushrooms at midnight from the Jabberwock's cave

Fry them in a pan the size of Wembley Stadium

Toast muffins using the flaming breath of a wild dormouse

Pour tea for Tweedledum and the Mad Hatter using
    mock turtle milk

Serve on a tray made out of butterfly wings.

'But that's seven,' said Alice.

'Yes,' said the poet. 'Poems can be very naughty sometimes.'

Silly Old Cat

A silly old cat from South Ealing
Liked to sleep on all paws on the ceiling.
She would snore and snore
Then fall to the floor
With a roar we thought most unappealing.

The Golden Retriever

On holiday last year in Geneva
Aunt Eva bought a golden retriever.
'It can retrieve hidden gold!'
Was the story she told
But no one, of course, would believe 'er.

Midnight in the Ice Rink

It is midnight in the ice rink
And all is cool and still.
Darkness seems to hold its breath
Nothing moves, until

Into the empty arena
The naughty pair come creeping.
They slink to the brink of the ice
While all the world is sleeping.

At first they're high-speed skaters.
Round and round they race
Blades hissing, sissing,
All at a dizzy pace

Now they're Olympic dancers
Pirouetting on the spot.
Fearless, they take no chances
As they slip and giggle a lot.

All night long the fun goes on
Until the sun, their friend,
Gives the warning signal
That all good things must end.

So yawning and smiling
they creep back to the house,
Torvill the ginger kitten
And her partner, Dean the mouse.

Three Cheers for the Cheerleaders

Who cheers up the cheerleaders
when their team has lost the game?
When the star wide receiver
has suddenly gone lame?

Who cheers up the cheerleaders
when the cheerful mask slips?
Wipes the tears of the running back
when he stumbles and trips?

Who cheers up the cheerleaders
when the home fans hiss and boo?
Makes the tight ends giggle
when they're feeling sad and blue?

Who cheers up the cheerleaders
when they're down in the dumps?
Gently rubs liniment
into the quarterback's lumps?

Who cheers up the cheerleaders' leader
when her pom-pom is snatched by a crow?
(Probably one of the linebackers.
To be honest I really don't know.)

But I do know how much we shall miss them
after the game when they slip away
So three hearty cheers for the cheerleaders
Hip hip . . . hip hip . . . hooray!

The Poetry Olympics

Nervous but quietly confident
The poem is up at first light.
The big day, after years of dreaming,
Has finally arrived. The end is in sight.

It runs, it jumps, it rides, it drives.
It rows, it throws, it collides, it dives.
It kicks, it flicks, it cycles, it swerves.
It lifts, it shifts, it aims, it serves.

It scans, it puzzles, it echoes, it chimes.
It struts, it performs, it sings, it rhymes.
One more line and it's complete.
The dreaming is over – now it's time to compete.

Tobogganing in Tobago

Toboggans in Tobago are plentiful and cheap
Not for sliding downhill but for surfing the deep

Prized by teenagers who take to the seas
barrelling the waves with breath-taking ease

Old timers wobble on second-hand skis
as toddlers doggy-paddle down on their knees

Out on the ocean doing just as they please
those happy-go-lucky Tobagonese.

Granma's Gooseberry Jam

What made me become
The man that I am?
Granma's gooseberry jam

It brightens our days.
Let's all sing in praise
Of amazing gooseberry jam

Gooseberry jam, gooseberry jam
Her sweet, soggy, goosegoggy gooseberry jam

Wherever you are
Spoon it straight from the jar.
It goes great with a plate of roast lamb.

It even puts into shade
Her granmarmalade,
This magical gooseberry jam.

Gooseberry jam, gooseberry jam
Her sweet, soggy, goosegoggy gooseberry jam

Her cherry's delicious,
Her damson's nutritious,
Her strawberry's out of this world,

But the sweet tangy juice
From the fruit of the goose
Is the secret of Grandmother's jam.

Gooseberry jam, gooseberry jam
Her sweet, soggy, goosegoggy gooseberry jam.

The geese are all itchin'
To flock to her kitchen
And be made into gooseberry jam.

So join in the chorus
There's nowt better for us
Than Granma's gooseberry jam.

Gooseberry jam, gooseberry jam
Her sweet, soggy, goosegoggy gooseberry jam.
Gooseberry jam, gooseberry jam
Her sweet, soggy, goosegoggy gooseberry jam.

Rich

Does money grow on trees, Mum?
I sometimes wish it would.
To shake some off when we need it?
Now wouldn't that be good?

Money is not there for the taking
And not there to waste or burn
It's something that needs looking after
A skill you'll have to learn.

You give your time and effort
And someone in return
Will pay you back with money
So while you work you earn.

Grandad gave me 50p
Just for being quiet.
If that's what earning is,
Then everyone should try it.

Well, Grandad's Grandad, as you know
But as a general rule
Earning means working hard
Like doing well at school

And doing jobs for people
That help them make a living.
Earning is not about taking;
It's really more about giving.

Can I be rich and buy a huge house?
Drive round in a classy car?
You have family, friends and a big, big smile.
Rich? You already are.

Money-go-round

Money-go-round, money-go-round
In for a penny, in for a pound
Money-go-round, money-go-round
Don't spend too much time on the money-go-round

There's a lesson to be learned and the message is clear
If you fall in love with money, it can soon disappear
Your dreams will get too big and then crash to the ground
If you spend too much time on the money-go-round

It can drive you crazy if it gets out of hand
For things don't always turn out exactly as you'd planned
When you're dizzy with the whizzing and the spinning around
It's time to say goodbye to the money-go-round

Money-go-round, money-go-round
In for a penny, in for a pound
Money-go-round, money-go-round
Don't spend too much time on the money-go-round.

Now You Are Grown-up

You are grown-up when you realize

That things go on working and moving without you
In your absence days out and parties go with a swing
Planes and trains arrive in cities you will never visit

That socks do not wash themselves
That a dream is just that, a dream
That wishing with all your might makes no difference

You are grown-up when you realize

That a hundred per cent is out of the question
That your best will never quite be good enough
That sometimes it may be wiser not to own up

Whether you are five, forty-five or one hundred and five
Congratulations – now you are grown-up.

When You Grow Up

One morning Teacher said to the class,
'Listen carefully, I am going to ask a question,
then one by one I want you to stand up
and give me the answer. The question is:
What do you want to be when you grow up?'

One by one we stood up and gave an answer.
(What would yours have been?)
'A nurse' said one, 'a doctor' said another,
'a ballet dancer', 'a soldier', 'a footballer',
'a film star', 'a unicorn!' (*That's what she said.*)

And so on until everybody had answered.
Except me. I thought it was a trick question
and Teacher was waiting for the correct answer.
'When I grow up,' I said, 'I want to be older.'
The class looked at me as if I was stupid.

'That's not what I meant,' said Teacher,
giving them all a chance to burst out laughing.
But I wasn't trying to be funny or clever.
I just wanted to be truthful. (*Plus the fact that
I had no idea what I wanted to be when I grew up.*)

And now that I have long since left school
but kept in touch with a few classmates,
I know that Sheila became a nurse, and Don
joined the army, but there were no doctors,
ballet dancers, film stars and certainly no unicorns.

Although most, but not all, like me grew older.

Let Us Know*

If your mum gives you an earful
And your best friend makes you tearful
If you're feeling sad and low
Let us know, let us know, let us know

If you can't help overspending
And boredom seems never-ending
Don't let your worries grow
Let us know, let us know, let us know

We'll make you feel much better
Because that's our *raison d'être***
(If you don't know what that means
Let us know, let us know, let us know)

If your skating skills are lacking
And the ice below starts cracking
We're here and quick to go
Let us know, let us know, let us know

So smile when the wind starts blowin'
And laugh when it's cold and snowin'
Let all your worries go
Let it snow, let it snow, let it snow
Let it snow, let it snow, let us know.

* To the tune of 'Let it Snow'.
** A French word meaning duty, aim in life, etc.

The Last Christmas Tree

I'm the last tree standing
All the rest have been sold
If nobody wants me
I'll be thrown out in the cold.

'Look, Mum, there's one left
In the corner by the wall
Its branches are all droopy
And it's not very tall.'

'Better than nothing,'
said Mum, 'I suppose.
It's Christmas day tomorrow
and the shop's about to close.

And the thought of it being
chucked out into the snow . . .
We wouldn't like that, would we?
So let's buy it and go.'

Phew! thought the tree
I may be scraggy and small
But thanks to these kind people
I won't be lonely at all.

And this little tree, I can guarantee
Knows how to put on a show
When drizzled in silver and fairy lights
I will grow and grow and grow!

The Veggie Table

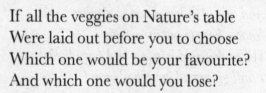

If all the veggies on Nature's table
Were laid out before you to choose
Which one would be your favourite?
And which one would you lose?

A crispy Cabbage, Spring or Savoy?
Its Chinese cousin the Pak Choi?
Carrots loaded with vitamin C?
Peas are fun, I bet you agree?

Turnips seem to be out of fashion
But chefs love Parsnips with a passion.
Corn on the cob will rarely fail.
Crunchy Celery or curly Kale?

The Potato, boiled, mashed or fried?
Butternut squash, all squishy inside?
Shiny Onions dangling on a string?
Garlic, small but packs a zing?

Cauliflower? Courgette? Aubergine?
In Tomato sauce the good old Bean?
Avocado? Red Pepper? Have I left one out?
Cucumber? Lettuce? Have I left one out?
Please tell me, have I left one out?

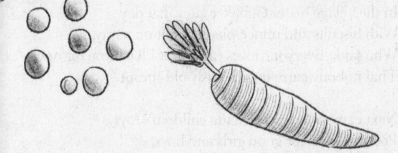

Teacher told me that technically courgettes, aubergines, tomatoes, avocados, peppers and cucumbers are fruits not vegetables, but do I care? I'm a poet not a greengrocer.

The Runaway Sprout

Christmas was coming, the season of good cheer,
But not for this little vegetable, I fear,
Who had escaped that morning from the farm.
Freedom beckoned but he tried to keep calm.

And as he rolled along he considered his fate.
There must be more to Christmas than a heaped-up plate?
Would he find friends to help him out?
To provide food and shelter for a runaway sprout?

In the village he met a baker later that day
With biscuits and mince pies laid out on a tray,
Who said, 'Everyone loves cakes, but I'll tell you for nowt
That nobody cares for a measly old sprout.'

Next came a lady who made children's toys,
Presents ideal for good girls and boys,
Who said, 'Kiddies love gifts, but could well do without
The presence at Christmas of a boring old sprout.'

A burly woodcutter carrying a tree
Said, 'Add fairy lights and I guarantee
There'll be magic this Christmas, but without a doubt
Nobody but nobody wants a wrinkly old sprout.'

(This poem is so sad – all he wanted was fun.
To be treated so cruelly, what harm had he done?)
But he carried on bravely, undeterred,
For the Boy Sprout's motto is *Be Prepared*.

Then a voice said, 'Come and join us,' inviting him in.
'Take a seat – the party is about to begin.'
Mrs Claus it was, with a smile a mile wide.
'Welcome, lad, and guess who's waiting inside?'

He looked at the crowd and who should he see
But the baker, the toymaker and the man with the tree
Who winked and smiled and made a right fuss.
'We were joking,' they said, ''cos you're one of us.'

With Santa at its centre the room was full.
There were gifts and games and crackers to pull.
Sharing and caring that's what it's about
For at Christmas no one is ever left out.
So let's all give three cheers for the runaway sprout!

The Christmas Sound Collector

The Sound Collector hated sounds,
Ones that filled the world with joy.
'Silence will be the gift I bring
To every girl and boy.'

He bought some scraggy reindeer
And hired a second-hand sleigh,
Cried, 'Look out, kids, I'm coming!'
Then upped and flew away

He went from house to house
Dressed all in grey and black,
Took every sound that could be found
And stuffed it in his sack

The fluttering of the snowflakes
The whisper of the breeze
The whirring of the wings
Of robins in the trees

The ringing of the church bells
The singing of the choirs
The clinking of the glasses
The crackling of the fires

The pulling of the crackers
The popping of the corks
The tingle and the tinkle
of impatient knives and forks

The unwrapping of the presents
The screaming of the kids
The bubbling of the saucepans
The rattle of the lids

The spluttering of the candles
The carollers at the door
Her Majesty on the telly
Granny's loud contented snore

And he surely would have succeeded
With his sneaky selfish crime
If Santa hadn't noticed
And got there just in time.

Santa Claus was feeling weary
After his busiest night of the year
And was on the point of returning home
When he noticed in his ear . . .

Nothing!
Silence hung like a threat in the air.
Something sinister he suspected
Was happening down there.

Needing to investigate,
He reined in the reindeer. 'Whoa!'
Then with sleepy eyes scrutinized
The town that lay below.

One house stood out.
It was the absence of noise that drew him.
He surprised the sneak thief on the roof
And with all his strength he threw him . . .

                              . . . to the ground.

The spell at last was broken
And to everyone's delight
The sack burst open and the sounds
Of Christmas filled the night.

The crackling of the telly
The snoring of the choirs
The popping of the robins
The ringing of the fires

The hissing of the knives and forks
The tinkling of the snow
The clinking of the carollers
when time for them to go

The fluttering of Granny's glasses
The spluttering of the lids
The bubbling of Her Majesty
The unwrapping of the kids

The cursing of the Sound Collector
As he upped and flew away
The hubbub and the laughter.
The magical sounds of Christmas day!

The Closing Poem

This is the closing poem
The last one in the book
So before you put it down
Here's one more for good luck

This is the closing poem
Bringing down the final curtain
No more verses hiding away
Of that you can be certain

This is the closing poem
To say thank you and goodbye
Writing makes you feel better
So why not give it a try?

Acknowledgements

For the poem 'Let Us Know' grateful acknowledgement is made to the songwriters of 'Let It Snow', Sammy Cahn and Jule Styne.

'The Runaway Sprout' comes from an idea by the RKCR group for a BBC animation film advert.

Author Acknowledgements

I wish to thank my editor, Helen Levene, the team at Puffin and my copy-editor Jennie Roman, Emily Talbot at United Agents and Adrian Mealing at UK Touring.

I would also like to acknowledge the work done by CLPE (Centre for Literacy in Primary Education), Action for Children's Arts, the Poetry Society and all the organizations who stress the importance of poetry when bringing up our children.

Index of Poems

Alphabet Soup 46

Angel in the Library, An 50

Anybody There? 63

At Home on the Range 56

Badger Dreams of That Final Bout, The 30

Battle of Trafalgar Square, The 42

Beating the Bugs 75

Cat Dreams of Becoming a Racing Driver, The 26

Cautionary Tale, A 62

Christmas Sound Collector, The 108

Closing Poem, The 113

DIY Valentine Card 64

Drums on Legs 78

Everyday Birthday Day 66

Feeble Excuses 68

Few Questions About Eternity, A 72

Golden Retriever, The 85

Good Ship *Attenborough*, The 44

Granma's Gooseberry Jam 92

Haiku Hygiene 15

Hooked on Haiku 14

I Am Done with Shade 77

I'm Nicer Than I Look 80

I'm Not as Nice as I Look 81

Last Christmas Tree, The   102
Let Us Know   100
Midnight in the Ice Rink   86
Mischief and Beans   38
Money-go-round   96
More Alphabet Soup, Anyone?   49
My First Haiku   12
My Second Haiku   13
No Going Back   17
Nonner   76
Not So Well After Dark   61
Now You Are Grown-up   97
Once Upon a Bicycle   34
Opening Poem, The   1
Out There   58
Perfect Day, The   65
Performance Poet   57
Poem to Help Make the World a Better Place, A   9
Poetry Olympics, The   90
Puzzle Tree, The   70
Rabbit Dreams of the Open Seas, The   28
Rhinoceros Dreams of Becoming an Airline Pilot, The   25
Rich   94
Runaway Sprout, The   106
Schlimmbesserung   11
Silly Old Cat   84
Six Impossible Things to Do Before Breakfast   82

Skip Skip Hooray!   41
Starfish *Enterprise*   39
This Poem is Punishment   8
This Was Meant to Be My Final Poem   20
Three Cheers for the Cheerleaders   88
Tobogganing in Tobago   91
Today I Am Writing a New Poem   18
Today I Am Writing My First Poem   5
Today I Am Writing My Second Poem   6
Today I Am Writing My Third Poem   7
Today I Found a Simile on the Carpet   10
Today I Will Finish the Poem I Started Yesterday   19
Veggie Table, The   104
Vlad the Impala   40
Wasp Speaks Out in Defence, The   32
Well After Dark   60
Well-mannered Poetry   52
When You Grow Up   98
Who Was the Girl?   36
Wild Stallions   54
Without Eternity Where Are We?   74
Word of Warning about Words, A   16

Index of First Lines

A nonner, what a nonner   76

A silly old cat from South Ealing   84

A starfish stranded upon the shore   39

A word of warning   14

After reading this   15

Answers are Questions' best friends (until they get one
    wrong)   46

Be warned: today I feel strong and agile   38

Christmas was coming, the season of good cheer   106

Cover your mouth when you cough   75

Does money grow on trees, Mum?   94

For homework I have to write a poem   10

Give a word an inch and it will take a mile   16

Give an antelope a skipping rope   41

How quiet was it before the Big Bang?   72

I am done with shade   77

I am writing my second poem   6

I am writing my third poem   7

I am writing this poem   8

I dream of Monte Carlo   26

I had alphabet soup for lunch   49

I may be hairy and smelly   80

I may look nice on the cover   81

I wanted to write a poem   9

I wish my poems used bad language 52
If all the veggies on Nature's table 104
If *Eternity* 74
If I could choose, what tree would I be? 70
If your mum gives you an earful 100
I'm sorry this card arrived so late . . . 68
I'm the last tree standing 102
I'm Vlad the Impala 40
It is midnight in the ice rink 86
It was a disappointing day all round 65
It was my birthday yesterday 66
Make fresh orange juice using only lemons and Jaffa
 Cakes 82
Money-go-round, money-go-round 96
Nervous but quietly confident 90
Not an astronaut or a scientist 57
Now you wouldn't think to look at me 30
On holiday last year in Geneva 85
Once upon a bicycle 34
Once you start writing poems 17
One morning Teacher said to the class 98
Poetry should have good manners 52
Sailing, they say, is a wonderful life 28
So far, so good 18
So far, so good, as far as I can tell 19
The 25
The books in the library 50

The Sound Collector hated sounds   108
There are times when I feel I'm not real   63
There is something strange about Trafalgar Square   42
There's excitement in Antarctica   44
This haiku was closed   13
This is the closing poem   113
This is the first time   12
This is the opening poem   1
This morning I threw caution to the wind   62
This was meant to be my final poem   20
Thursday evening, well after dark   61
TO_____   64
Toboggans in Tobago are plentiful and cheap   91
Today I am writing my first poem   5
Wednesday evening, well after dark   60
What is it like out there?   58
What made me become   92
When I'm dancing   78
Who cheers up the cheerleaders   88
Who was the naughty girl I saw   36
Words running wild don't make sense   56
Yesterday Teacher made the class   11
You are grown-up when you realize   97
Z-Z-z-sorry I stung you. I don't know what it is   32

More poetry to enjoy by
Roger McGough